Walt Disney's

DISNEYLAND

by Martin A. Sklar

THE BEHIND-THE-SCENES STORY OF THE MAGIC KINGDOM
...OF THE MAN WHO MADE IT POSSIBLE,
...AND OF THE MILLIONS OF VISITORS WHO HAVE HELPED
MAKE IT THE HAPPIEST PLACE ON EARTH

"To all who come to this happy place: welcome. Disneyland is your land. Here age relives fond memories of the past... and here youth may savor the challenge and promise of the future.

"Disneyland is dedicated to the ideals, the dreams and the hard facts which have created America... with the hope that it will be a source of joy and inspiration to all the world."

The spirit of Disneyland is embodied in these words, inscribed on the dedication plaque for the Magic Kingdom. It is located at the base of the flagpole in Town Square on Main Street, where a visit to Disneyland begins. At the other end of Main Street is the Plaza, center of Disneyland; here, fanning out like the spokes of a wheel, the entrances to each of the Park's "lands" are located.

To walk from Town Square, down Main Street, and through each of these realms is to travel only a mile and a quarter. But that distance is measured not in steps or in hours; it is measured in personal experiences. Those who come to Disneyland call upon the whole spectrum of imagination to respond anew to those ideals, dreams and hard facts which are our heritage.

The Impossible is Fun

Lining the walls of WED Enterprises where designers create new attractions for Disneyland, sketches, plot plans and huge aerial photographs detail the future of the Magic Kingdom. Here visitors, who often include international dignitaries, the world press, and representatives of American industry, preview what is to come at the Park. For years art directors, touring these guests past dreams that are to become realities, have pointed to a map marked for expansion and casually, as though savoring some delicious private joke, explained: "And here, Walt's thinking about enlarging the Grand Canyon."

Like Disneyland itself, the humor has mellowed with age. Somewhere along the years, the quizzical, who-do-you-think-you're-kidding glances have disappeared. Today visitors simply nod in knowing appreciation. For no one but Walt Disney ever *thought* of recreating a Grand Canyon in the first place. And he *has,* in fact, enlarged it.

Walt Disney often refers to the diverse entertainment bearing his name as a team accomplishment. At WED Enterprises (the initials WED are those of its founder, Walter E. Disney), the continuing search for new ideas and the unique application of these ideas has been called "imagineering."

To Walt Disney and his team participating in its many facets—design, architecture, engineering, sculpting, electronics, music, costuming, landscaping, construction and many more —imagineering is a fascinating adventure. It is a stimulating challenge, a symphony of many arts and crafts, a harmonic blending of varied talents and skills. It is a "marriage," not of expediency but of creativity—the joining together of imagination in entertainment with the practical, expanding know-how of the engineer, the architect and the scientist.

The imagination and the special skills of this team have brought laughter and song, drama, and adventure to audiences in entertainment ranging from motion pictures to television, and from Disneyland to the New York World's Fair.

Yet from its very beginnings, Disneyland was considered by many to be an "impossible" project, a "reckless gamble." How Disneyland grew from a persistent dream to a prodigious reality is the story in this book. That Disneyland succeeded is due to the man who had that dream. To Walt Disney, the impossible has always been "kind of fun."

The Many Worlds of Disneyland

In all the world, there is but one Disneyland. In a decade's time, 55 million guests have come here from the earth's four corners, each to participate in adventures unique in all the world. For here, tomorrow is today, and yesterday is forever.

In all the world, there is but one Disneyland. Yet Disneyland is many different worlds. It is 1890 again on Main Street, U.S.A. and 1980 in Tomorrowland. It is the pioneer's hardy world, Frontierland, and a jungle safari to far-off places in Adventureland. And it is a castle full of dreams—the classic tales of childhood "come to life" in Fantasyland.

But Disneyland is far more than medieval castles and twentieth-century rocket ships, horse-drawn streetcars and monorail trains,

the children who telephone to ask, "Can I speak to Mickey Mouse?" and the telephone operators who answer, "I'm sorry, he's taking his nap now." It is a teenager aboard an 1850 sternwheeler on a moonlit night, seeking an introduction to a girl by asking: "Is this your first trip abroad?" And it is an ambassador telling newsmen, "Disneyland is for kids... kids like you and me."

Disneyland is active participation in personal adventures that stimulate the imagination. A middle-aged lady about to "blast-off" for the moon suddenly leaves her rocket ship seat and rushes to the hostess, exclaiming: "I've got to get off—I'm afraid of getting air sick!" A little girl "submerged" aboard a submarine hears the captain announce that the vessel is "beneath the North Pole" and excitedly asks her daddy, "Will we see Santa Claus?" Thirty-five passengers turn their heads in unison as the "native guide," piloting a launch into the teeming jungles of Adventureland, suggests, "Take a last look at the dock—you may never see it again!"

Disneyland is the complete absence of the tawdry "carney" barker. In his place is the smiling "Disneylander": the grey-haired man who makes sure your child's feet are securely fastened in the stirrups on a frisky mule; the bubble-helmeted "spaceman" patiently answering questions about "his world"; the pretty tour guide who admits she doesn't know the answer to your question, but promises to mail the information to your home—and does.

Disneyland is the sign in a glassware shop on Main Street, "Relax. We Don't Charge for Accidental Breakage," and another sign at Main Street's City Hall, "Lost Parents, Inquire Here for Children."

jungle elephants and elephants that fly, snow-capped mountains and colorful deserts.

What is Disneyland? It is the innocence of youth and the wisdom of age. It is a child examining the hitching posts that line an 1890 street and asking "Mommy, what kind of parking meters are these?" It is an elderly gentleman on the same street, smiling happily as he tells a bystander what he likes best about Disneyland: "I can jaywalk here." It is

Disneyland is people forgetting their everyday cares and immersing themselves in the worlds of fantasy and adventure, yesterday and tomorrow—but no today. It is the late King Mohammed V of Morocco departing after an official visit, then eluding State Department escorts to see Disneyland a second time in one afternoon. It is former President Eisenhower treating son John's youngsters to a day of fun like any other grandfather. It is Supreme Court Chief Justice Earl Warren dropping in unannounced late one afternoon "because everywhere I travel in the world people ask me about Disneyland." It is the Prime Minister of Pakistan, watching the old west show in Frontierland, receiving a direct hit from the

comedian's water pistols—and laughing.

You find the magic of Disneyland in the soft pastel lighting of Sleeping Beauty Castle as evening approaches; in the twinkling eyes of a grandfather wearing an orange-billed Donald Duck hat; in a child kissing a life-size Mickey Mouse while Dad fumbles with his camera; in hard penny candy at the Market House and leeches in jars at the turn-of-the-century apothecary; in kids following the band as it parades up Main Street playing a Sousa march; in secret passages in rock formations on Tom Sawyer Island—just big enough for kids to squeeze through, but far too small for a middle-aged spread.

Disneyland is the emotion that wells up within you when the *Mark Twain* stern-

wheeler steams 'round the bend twinkling with sparklers from bow to stern, as Louis Armstrong leads 50 Dixieland jazz musicians in the classic "When the Saints Go Marching In." Disneyland is a Christmas Parade with dozens of Disney characters performing as they march the length of Main Street and circle the Plaza. It is teenagers emulating pretzels as they twist away a summer evening, while Mom and Dad turn over an old leaf to fox-trot and jitterbug and just listen to the time-honored sounds of the "big bands": Count Basie, Duke Ellington, Harry James, Benny Goodman. Disneyland is fireworks bursting over a castle on a summer night, and the boastful Texan who claims, "Those were fine, but we have 'em bigger down where I come from." And the quiet little lady standing next to him who smiles and asks, "Every night?"

But most of all, the spirit of Disneyland is found in the story of the boy who got his first real job at the age of 15, as a "news butcher" selling peanuts, candy, magazines and apples to people riding on trains between Kansas City and Chicago. Today you sometimes see him in the cab of an 1870 steam locomotive, taking its throttle for a trip around Disneyland. Walt Disney still loves to tinker—with old trains, and new ideas.

They Said It Couldn't Be Done

In the Minneapolis *Tribune* shortly after Disneyland opened, Will Jones wrote: "If it's an amusement park, it's the gosh-darnedest, most happily-inspired, most carefully-planned, most adventure-filled park ever conceived. No ride or concession in it is like anything in any other amusement park anywhere."

Disneyland, obviously, was never meant to be an "amusement park." The new concept in entertainment dedicated in Disneyland on July 17, 1955, was much more. The Magic Kingdom is a fabulous playground—something of a fair, a city from the Arabian Nights, a metropolis of the future. Above all, it is a place for people to find happiness and knowledge.

When Disneyland opened in Anaheim (27 miles southeast of downtown Los Angeles), it was a 20-year dream come true for its creator, chief architect and head imagineer, Walt Disney. Rough drawings for a "Disneyland" had been found at the Disney studio dating back to the early 1930's, less than five years after Mickey Mouse made his film debut. "I was always trying to think of a place to take my two small daughters on a Saturday or Sunday afternoon—a place where *I* could have fun too," Walt told the *Reader's Digest*. "At an amusement park the only fun provided for a father, besides having his bottom dropped out from under him on the roller coaster, was the same he enjoyed all week: buying the tickets."

So Walt Disney began to dream, and to plan, a new kind of entertainment center for the young at heart of all ages. But the concept that emerged in the 1950's bore little resemblance to the small park Walt had first envisioned.

Members of his staff recall Walt talking about building an intimate little park adjacent to his Burbank studio. It was to be a "magical little park" two acres in size, with train and pony rides, "singing waterfalls" and statues dedicated to the motion picture characters people throughout the world were

already accepting as their own — Mickey Mouse, of course, and Donald Duck, Pluto, Goofy and the rest. It was to be a place to take visitors during tours of the studio and where studio employees might spend relaxing weekends with their families.

The concept never really took hold, however. For there is a basic truism that governs every success that bears the name Disney: no idea remains very long in its original form. Walt is a builder; his basic materials are ideas. He works with them, plays with them, grows with them, and finally — perhaps years after they first find expression — ideas emerge as tangible realities in motion pictures, television or Disneyland.

For years the "Disneyland" project lay dormant. World War II intervened, and Mickey Mouse, Donald Duck and their friends "enlisted," to star in a variety of training and morale films viewed by millions of GI's. But Disneyland was far from forgotten.

The man who remembered it has often been called "a creative genius who has the capacity to make his dreams come true." Walt Disney's close associates refer to this "touch of the genie" as an inborn instinct for communicating with people through entertainment.

"It's as though Walt had a crystal ball," says a Disney executive. "If the bankers, or other people in show business don't know what he's driving at, Walt just figures they don't understand—and goes right ahead with his newest idea because he personally believes in it. He's never off on 'cloud nine', yet he never does something merely because he thinks it will be a commercial success. Every project has to be one that Walt himself feels will be fun to create."

Disneyland was one of those far-out ideas that few people other than Walt Disney believed in. One of those who had faith in the idea was Walt's older brother Roy, president of Walt Disney Productions. *Newsweek* once reported that "to build Disneyland Walt and Roy Disney borrowed to the corporate hilt, and then Walt sold his vacation home at a loss and borrowed against his personal life insurance policies."

Collectively, some of the more indifferent and reserved groups toward the concept of Disneyland were the nation's amusement park owners and operators. Early in 1954, four key members of the Disney staff assigned to develop ideas for Disneyland toured the major permanent amusement parks across America. Recalls one: "We could have paid for the trip with a few dollars from everyone who told us, 'If you don't put in a roller coaster and a ferris wheel, you'll go broke'. Most were completely indifferent—especially the equipment manufacturers who had been building the same whips and shoot-the-chutes for years. They wanted us to buy what they already had, but Walt had other plans. I can only remember two or three of the long-time amusement operators who offered any kind of encouragement at all."

It must have come as a shock to the amusement park men to hear that the baseball throw and the tunnel of love were relics of the past as far as Disneyland was concerned. And to imagine a park without barkers was like thinking of a movie without sound.

In the final analysis, it was television which made Disneyland a reality. Just when all doors appeared to be closed, Walt Disney Productions and the American Broadcasting Com-

Disneyland, the television show, made its debut in the fall of 1954. Disneyland the Park opened less than a year later.

There were many times during those 12 months of construction when the stumbling blocks had appeared insurmountable. One man recalls tagging the orange trees to be retained with strips of red paper and those to be removed with green. A color-blind bulldozer operator began to fell the precious trees marked "save."

A construction supervisor remembers his glow of pride as water flowed into the Rivers of America in Frontierland for the first time ... then his feeling of desperation as the river promptly leaked its contents into the sandy soil of the former orange grove. Loads of clay soil had to be trucked in to waterproof the leaking river.

pany signed a seven-year contract that called for Walt to produce a weekly, one-hour television show. At the studio, its name had already been selected. The program would be called "Disneyland."

With the grand opening of Disneyland just two weeks away, more than 2,500 workmen were swarming over the land in two shifts that totaled 17 working hours a day. In this frantic setting, a television crew began positioning its cameras and rehearsing the scenes that would introduce Disneyland to America. The producer paled and hesitated as his gaze wandered over a scene where clouds of dust billowed and shifted as men and machines toiled. A Disney staff member stepped into the breach. "Don't worry," he comforted, "You'll have plenty of action to shoot. We'll be pouring cement!"

When Disneyland at last opened to an eagerly awaiting public, a mine train pulled out of its station in Frontierland, its load of contemporary pioneers comfortably seated in railway cars designed to recall those that once emerged brimming with silver ore from the mountain tunnels of the west. As the engineer headed his locomotive toward the buttes and rock formations in the distance, he told a little story to his passengers: "A few years ago, this was all row after row of orange trees. Today... cactus, snakes, sagebrush, desert. *That's* progress for you!"

A Los Angeles newspaper, quoting an unidentified diplomat, recently reported: "All the crowned heads of Europe want to see Disneyland." Most of them already have: a dozen kings and queens, 18 presidents and prime ministers, 29 princes and princesses, and even a few premiers—with one notable exception. By staying away, that one exception splashed his name, and Disneyland's, across the front pages of newspapers around the world. His name: Nikita S. Khrushchev.

In September, 1960, Disneyland became the center of a *cause célèbre* when the then-Soviet Premier startled millions of television viewers—and his American State Department escorts—by denouncing the evils of our capitalistic society in a novel way. It had, he said in effect, barred him from having a bit of fun because too many security precautions were necessary before he could visit Disneyland. The "international incident" set off quite a chain reaction:

*Author Herman Wouk wrote a letter: "I don't blame Khrushchev for jumping up and down in rage over missing Disneyland. There are few things more worth seeing in the United States, or indeed anywhere in the world."

*Bob Hope told a joke: "Here we are in Alaska, our 50th state. Alaska—that's halfway between Khrushchev and Disneyland."

*Mr. K. himself soon had an announcement: The Soviet Union, he said, planned to build a "country of miracles" park. Or, as the Moscow park would be called, "Miracleland."

*And in New York City the day following the Soviet Premier's complaint heard 'round the world, an officer of one of capitalism's largest brokerage houses telephoned a Disney executive. The Californian recalls the conversation:

"Maybe you don't remember me," the voice from the east coast said. "I'm the one who said we don't finance 'kiddylands' when you were looking for money to build Disneyland. Now I want to visit your place; if Khrushchev can get so mad over *not* seeing it, Disneyland can't be much of a kiddyland!"

Not an amusement park...certainly not a kiddyland. What then *was* the idea behind the creation of Disneyland? And who was qualified to design and shape this new medium of entertainment?

For the team that would help him build Disneyland, Walt Disney turned not to the experienced, skeptical amusement park operators. He turned instead to the field he knows best, motion pictures, and hand-picked a staff of artists, story tellers, machinists and special effects men unique not only for their skills... but for their wide-open eyes and minds.

At first consideration, the two mediums—indoor movies and outdoor entertainment—seem incompatible. But an art director who lived those hectic, formative days and nights has a ready explanation: "The basic premise in everything that went into Disneyland was participation, involving people in an experience, and—through that experience—evoking their emotions and stimulating their imaginations. Entertainment is basically an act of communication with an audience, whether that audience is a theater full of people or a mother and daughter in a pirate galleon flying over Peter Pan's moonlit London town."

Several years ago, writing in the New York *Times,* Gladwin Hill described this accomplishment in similar terms: "What is the success of Disneyland? Many factors have entered into it. But to pin-point a single element, it would be imagination—not just imagination on the part of its impresarios, but their evocation of the imagination of the cash customers. Walt Disney and his associates have managed to generate, in the traditionally raucous and ofttimes shoddy amusement-park field, the same 'suspension of disbelief' which has been the secret of theatrical success down the corridors of time...In the theatre, the vital ingredient is not realism, but a blending of the real with the imaginary. The entertainer invites the audience to meet him half way. That is what has been successfully achieved at Disneyland."

Writer Ray Bradbury also perceived imagination at work and play in Disneyland. In a letter to the editor published in *The Nation,* Bradbury described his first of many visits to Disneyland: "...I did better than take a child;...I accompanied one of the great theatrical and creative minds of our time, Charles Laughton. I've never had such a day

full of zest and high good humor. Mr. Laughton is no easy mark; he has a gimlet eye and searching mind. Yet *he* saw, and *I* found, in Disneyland, vast reserves of imagination before untapped in our country."

Some have likened Disneyland to a gigantic stage, upon which each guest moves about —seldom a spectator, often an actor participating in the unfolding drama—an integral part of the humor, the pathos, the verve of a new "theatre."

Added to the enormous task of blending all the ideas into a basic format for Disneyland was one more that posed the most difficult problem for its creators. Walt Disney wanted to design everything "new."

"Walt didn't want to build a new concept on old available ride machinery anyone could get his hands on," a construction designer recalls. "Almost everything we undertake in the Park has never been done before."

For example, designers working on the projected Rainbow Caverns envisioned a series of underground chambers with dazzling ribbons of water cascading down the walls of the caverns and flowing in streams of red, green, blue and yellow throughout the caves. To check the practicality of the plan, the artists called in a noted scientist. His report was gloomy. He proved that within a week all the rainbow colors would be but one— water-color gray. Walt listened to this dreary prediction, then turned to his associates and with a characteristic grin gave his own completely unscientific conclusion: "Well, it's kind of fun to do the impossible."

Six months later, the Rainbow Caverns opened at Disneyland. Today, years after their completion, visitors can pick out six distinct colors—none of them gray!

The "Lilly Belle" Grows Up

An engineer aboard the trains of the Santa Fe & Disneyland Railroad reports that the thunder and lightning storm inside the Grand Canyon diorama has a great many passengers thinking it's for real. "Almost every trip," he reports, "I see five or six people poke their arms out of the train windows to see if it's really pouring."

Imagination again...but imagination born out of realism that begins the moment visitors step aboard the trains of the Santa Fe & Disneyland Railroad. The detail and authenticity that characterize Disneyland may be said to take their cue from that railroad.

The *Lilly Belle*, a model train that once huffed and puffed around the back yard of Walt Disney's Holmby Hills home, was the prototype of the most letter-perfect 1890 railroad that ever whistled into a main street station. William McKinley and William Jennings Bryan on the campaign trail never had it better than the passengers of the Santa Fe & Disneyland taking a grand circle tour of the Magic Kingdom!

The tour includes stops at Frontierland and Tomorrowland, plus a journey through the Grand Canyon diorama. The most striking feature of the diorama is a 306-foot by 34-foot background painting, a seamless, hand-woven canvas that required 4,800 man-hours for painting alone. Appearing in a kaleidoscope of winter-to-spring and sunrise-to-sunset colors, the diorama gives viewers the feeling that they are peering into the Grand Canyon from its south rim.

In the months before Disneyland opened, two trains, an 1890 passenger and a western freight train, were constructed from the wheels

and pistons up in the machine shop at the Disney studio. Piece by piece, each train was painstakingly designed and assembled. Finely detailed woodwork, metal and iron work and most parts were individually crafted right in the Disney machine shop. The two locomotives built for Disneyland in 1954-55 were a "diamond stack" and a "cap stack," both 4-4-0 engines (they have four wheels in front, four drive wheels, and no trailing truck or tender).

There are now five trains on the railroad. One is pulled by a 70-year-old locomotive that once hauled cane sugar on the Lafourete Raceland and Longport Railway in Louisiana. It was located for the Park by the Railroad and Locomotive Historical Society.

Perhaps the most intriguing aspect of the trains' design was the manner in which scale was determined — and the resulting misconception, existing to this day, regarding the scale of buildings and other structures in Disneyland.

Walt's own *Lilly Belle,* 1/8 of full scale, was first "blown up" in drawings. Then a plywood "mock-up" was built, large enough for a man to walk through. When it was determined that a six foot door was adequate for a human passenger, the rest of the train followed in proportion. The size of the door dictated the size of the roof, the sides, and finally the wheels — 36 inches apart on the tracks, or almost exactly the same width as the narrow gauge railroads.

Standard railroad gauge is 56½ inches; Disneyland's 36-inch wheel spread is almost exactly 5/8 scale.

Popular notion is that all Disneyland is 5/8 scale. Actual fact is that only the trains, and some Disneyland vehicles such as the

antique autos on Main Street, are 5/8 scale. Main Street itself is several different scales: 9/10 of full size on the first floors of its buildings, and a scale smaller—8/10—at the second story level.

The Dream City

The real estate boom in a fantasy kingdom recently received a significant boost from a youngster in Peoria, Illinois. Scribbled the youth: "We are planning to move to Disneyland. Can you please send us some booklets about the rides and town?"

Many people have referred to Disneyland as a city unto itself. In a sense, Walt Disney's Magic Kingdom *is* a city...one with 4,500 "residents" (permanent and part-time employees) and more than six million visitors each year.

If Disneyland is to be called a city, it is one in which the major form of transportation is an imaginary "time machine." Whenever you step from this vehicle of the mind, you are in another age, another land—each one beckoning you to re-live the era, stories, hopes or dreams that it represents, and to participate in the varied entertainment within its own boundaries.

There are five such individual "kingdoms" within Disneyland: *Main Street, U.S.A.,* small-town America in the period 1890-1910, *Frontierland,* dedicated to the pioneering spirit and boisterous exploits of our forefathers, *Adventureland,* "the wonder world of nature's own design," with its jungle boat cruise to far-off lands, *Tomorrowland,* a prediction of things to come on the bold frontiers of the space age, and *Fantasyland,* the "happiest kingdom of them all," where classic stories of childhood have been brought to life.

In the summer of 1954, construction began on this 165 acre "city" in Anaheim. A year later, when Disneyland opened its gates to the public, two million board feet of lumber and 5,000 cubic yards of concrete had gone into its construction, and one million square feet of asphalt had paved its streets and walkways. Giant earth-movers and bulldozers had moved 350,000 cubic yards of earth—enough to build a 20-foot high berm, one and one-eighth miles long around the entire place. "I don't want the public to see the real world they live in while they're in the park," Walt Disney observed. "I want them to feel they are in another world."

After nearly 20 years, the "magical little park" had become a $17,000,000 magic kingdom. The dream had at last come true.

Main Street, U.S.A.

Disneyland's "time machine" begins to work the moment you walk onto Main Street, U.S.A. The contrast to the hustle and bustle of our modern world and its streamlined modes of transportation is sharp and penetrating. Suddenly, the entire mood changes, and the years roll backward—back to "anywhere in America," circa 1900. And *your* pace slows to match the leisurely clop-clop of the horse-drawn surrey, the um-pa-pa of a band concert in Town Square, the chug-chug of a horseless carriage.

Here once more is another age, rekindling fond memories or bringing to reality a page of Americana that previously existed only in a youngster's history books.

"Many of us fondly remember our small home town and its friendly way of life at the turn of the century," said Walt Disney. "To me, the era represents an important part of our heritage, and thus we have endeavored to recapture those years on Main Street, U.S.A. at Disneyland. Main Street represents the typical small town of the early 1900's—the heartline of America."

An art director recalls the philosophy that governed design of this Main Street: "There is a subtle difference between the small towns and large towns of any era. For example, Disneyland's bank and opera house would be out of place in a large city; but in our small town, they are right at home. We were striving to get the most character and flavor into the creation of Main Street. It was much like doing a set for a motion picture. The story-value had to be brought out to put people back in the 1890-1910 period."

There is, however, a not-so-subtle difference between the buildings that line Main Street and a movie set. The latter is to be seen but not touched or entered by the audience; the former is a world of sights and sounds—plus the sensations of touch and smell and the personal adventure of examining, shopping and inhaling the nectar of nostalgia.

From the shelves of Upjohn's apothecary lined with patent medicines that "cure everything from giddiness to trembling sensations," to the "white wing" whose shovel and receptacle were absolute essentials in an age when horses were inviolate (but not necessarily sanitary), Main Street has been authentically re-created.

The design of Main Street is typical of the complete researching that has always been the springboard for a Disneyland attraction. Hundreds of books, pictures and historical items were studied to get the feel of the interior and exterior of stores and shops of the 1900 era. A treasure hunt extended across the country into antique shops, private homes and out-of-the-way junk shops in small villages. The searchers tracked down relics of the past ranging from old lighting fixtures to the hitching posts of yesteryear.

What was found and brought back to Disneyland was the history of another age in bits and pieces. There were 100-year-old gas lamps from Baltimore and Philadelphia, grill work and railings from plantations in Nashville and Memphis, and small park benches from San Francisco.

This treasure contributes importantly to today's living of yesterday in Main Street's attractions, shops and exhibits: bank, bookstore, candle shop, market house, tobacconist, coffee house, ice cream parlor, photo display, registration and information center, china and glassware store, silhouette studio and City Hall. And, of course, the Cinema (silents only) where Rudolph Valentino is still "The Sheik" and hand-tinted slides graciously proclaim "Ladies Over 40 Need Not Remove Their Hats."

On Main Street, the horse and the "gasoline buggy," historic rivals, have become pals. Today teenagers sometimes laugh about "daddy's hot rod" and call the horse-drawn streetcars "hay-burning oatsmobiles." But in a land where the skilled touch of the artisan is seen on every side, Main Street's vehicles are truly works of art—in mechanized form.

To re-create a fire engine that might once have answered the alarm in a small village of 1900 America, the studio men designed a chassis, then pored through standard catalogs for unlikely but practical equipment: a jeep rear axle, a three-speed truck transmission, the power plant of a small pick-up truck, standard drive-line parts. To re-create a double-deck omnibus they used only *one* authentic part—an old electric klaxon horn. The drop frame chassis is from a modern day truck, and the bus has both power steering and power brakes! To build-in a slight case of the shakes for the horseless carriages, the designers used today's most efficient two-cylinder water pump engine.

Main Street's old-time autos might delight visitors, but there was a very good chance that they would scare the wits out of the ponies and Percherons who were to pull Disneyland's trolleys and surreys. So, in the weeks before the Park opened, the horses pranced around a circular ring for four hours each day while music, tooting automobile horns and the laughter and shouts of crowds blared at them from loudspeakers. Amid opening-day crowds, the animals felt right at home.

In an average year, Main Street's vehicles

travel more than 23,000 miles, up and down the avenue. Their destination is the Plaza, center of the Magic Kingdom—the stepping-off point for a journey into the many worlds of Disneyland.

Fantasyland

In medieval times, the drawbridge spanning a castle's moat was purely a defensive safeguard, cranked up to cut off an enemy's entry in time of attack. But when a castle with pink and blue parapets and towers became the entrance into the "happiest kingdom of them all," the drawbridge acquired a new meaning: it became the world's most unusual "welcome mat."

Beyond the drawbridge, in the broad courtyard of Sleeping Beauty Castle, classic stories of childhood are brought to life as adventures in participation for the young at heart. Some are outdoor attractions, for which the designers studied known principles of amusement park rides and adapted or completely revised them for new purposes. Others are Fantasyland's "dark rides," the indoor attractions in which black light, animation, sound and color effects are combined to create some of Disneyland's most beloved and beguiling entertainment.

Two decades of Disney motion picture entertainment provided the inspiration for the dark rides. From "Snow White and The Seven Dwarfs" came a trip through the Enchanted Forest and Diamond Mine. "Peter Pan" contributed a pirate galleon soaring high above the moonlit streets of London Town to Never-Never Land. Haughty caterpillar cars hurtle down the Rabbit Hole into the Upside Down Room, the Garden of Live Flowers, Tulgey Wood, and other settings from Alice's Wonderland. The "hot rodder" of storybook fable, J. Thaddeus (Mr.) Toad, emerges from "The Wind in the Willows" to topple barrels and frustrate policemen along the Road to Nowhere in Particular.

Fantasyland's outdoor attractions include the spinning, people-sized cups and saucers inspired by the Mad Hatter's tea party. Nearby, 72 steeds—each 60 to 80 years old and no two exactly alike—prance gaily to a calliope tune aboard the King Arthur Carousel, largest of its kind in the world. And while the Casey Jr. Circus Train still "thinks he can" climb that steep hill, Dumbo continues to make history as the world's only elephant with aerodynamic ears.

(Long-time Disneylanders still shudder recalling the day a subcontractor delivered the first herd of Dumbos. Specifications called for the elephants to be light-weight "shells" so that the mechanism could lift pachyderm and two guests high into the Fantasyland air. The first ones were indeed "baby elephants"— each weighing 700 pounds!)

The Castle itself is a composite of many medieval palaces, though its designers were probably most influenced by a Bavarian castle. Early drawings of the Disneyland Castle, in fact, looked so much like the German that the façade facing Main Street was extensively re-designed until today both Bavarian and French influences are present.

Though the Castle's tallest tower is but 77 feet above the moat, a device well-known in motion picture circles, forced perspective, has been used to trick the eye into telling the mind that the castle is much taller. The walls and battlements are constructed of stones cut in graduated sizes, from large ones at the foundation to small ones at the top-

most sentry posts and turrets.

The same visual trickery has been used in Disneyland's biggest attraction, Matterhorn Mountain. An exact 1/100th scale replica of its Alpine namesake, Disneyland's mountain is 145.6 feet high, but it appears much higher. Up, around and down its concrete and steel slopes (500 tons of structural steel, none exactly the same size) race four-passenger "bobsleds." Climax of a trip down the mountain is a splash into a pool of water at the base, thrilling the passengers—and stopping the bobsleds.

The mountain is pierced by a series of holes, through which the bobsleds race and trams of the Skyway glide on their airborne journey between Fantasyland and Tomorrowland. According to Disneyland legend, King Baudouin of Belgium is said to have asked Walt Disney why this Matterhorn has holes, and Disney is supposed to have answered, with perfect logic, "Because it's a Swiss mountain."

For perhaps the first time in history, landscapers were called upon to decide just exactly what constitutes "timberline" on a 14-story building. Halfway to the Matterhorn's "snow-capped" summit, they decided, and planted varieties of pine ranging in height from 12 feet at the bottom to two feet at timberline. Forced perspective again.

From the biggest to the smallest in Disneyland is a journey of just a few steps—to Storybook Land. Here European canal boats and the Casey Jr. Train whisk you away to a "kingdom within a kingdom," where the delicate touch of the model maker and the landscaper's inventiveness combine to portray settings in miniature from Disney animated motion pictures.

Model makers at the Disney studio labored six months turning artists' visualizations of Pinocchio's Village, the straw-stick-brick homes of the Three Little Pigs, and other fable favorites into detailed buildings, on a scale of one inch to one foot. They made lead hinges so that six-inch doors would actually open for electricians to change light bulbs. They carved dozens of tiny toys for the window of Gepetto's shop. They installed minute drain pipes and hand-crafted "stained glass" and leaded windows.

Then the landscapers moved in, matching the miniature dwellings by ingenious use of plants and flowers. First they selected plants whose leaf-size was but one-quarter to one-half inch, then they restricted root growth by planting in containers. They met special design problems: they pruned and shaped a three-foot tall Japanese boxwood with gnarled trunk to represent the oak tree where Alice entered the Rabbit Hole. They also uprooted a 100-year-old grape vine, turned it upside down and made it appear like the "terribly tortured old snag" in front of Ratty's home in "The Wind in the Willows."

The most difficult task was in finding live trees that would not *grow* any more, for the forest surrounding the home of the Seven Dwarfs. The answer to the problem seemed to be the Japanese *bonsai* tree. However, these tiny trees require constant care; poor trees were very expensive and good specimens were almost unobtainable. Near Mendocino, in northern California, the landscapers literally unearthed a much more perfect solution. Pine trees truly dwarfed in every respect were growing three to 12 feet in height in a "pygmy forest"—just 50 feet from the same species towering 60 to 80 feet tall! The

dwarfed trees had rooted in a limestone shelf; their growth rate is so slow it is nearly impossible to measure. A dozen of these trees now "grow" in Storybook Land, in soil closely matching the nearly sterile conditions of that limestone shelf.

Adventureland

"Walt Disney depleted our nurseries from Santa Barbara to San Diego," wrote Hedda Hopper on the eve of Disneyland's opening, and certainly no single project in memory taxed the commercial gardening trade as did Disneyland. Before construction began on the Park, the Disney acreage in Anaheim was almost entirely sandy-soiled orange groves. Today Disneyland is a botanical wonderland. Each year, 500,000 annual and perennial plants and flowers are planted and 1,000 trees transplanted to maintain springtime in the winter and showtime all year 'round. Nowhere is the landscaping more vital than in Adventureland, where a unique combination of living plants and life-like animals has reproduced the atmosphere of the world's tropic regions, from darkest Africa to densest Amazon. Almost overnight, the banks of Adventureland's river were made to overflow with trees, flowers and grasses indigenous to the tropics. Fortunately, southern California is a sub-tropical region; nearly all the jungle plant life was available from major nurseries and private gardens within a 200 mile radius of Anaheim.

Among the most unusual plants growing in Adventureland today are the rare "Bushman's poison," which provides venom for the arrow tips of African hunters; the sacred Bo Tree of India; taro, staple diet of many tropic

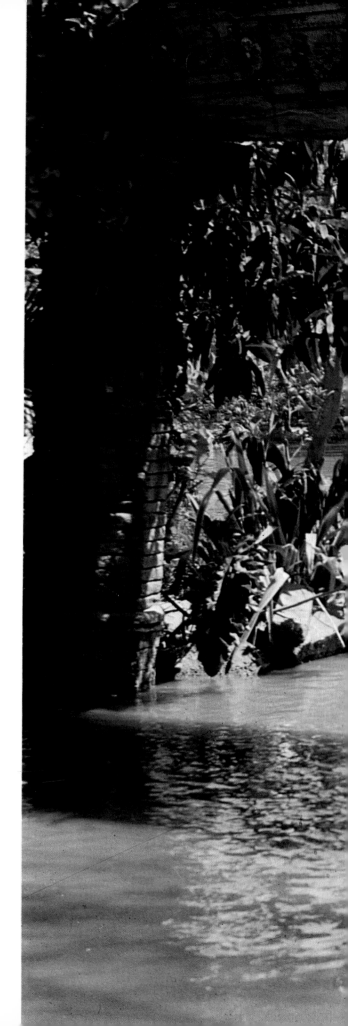

peoples; and timber-bamboo growing as high as 60 feet. Today the biggest problem for Disneyland landscapers is the same encountered in any untamed land of dense vegetation: controlling the tangle of vines and ferns that make up a true-to-life jungle.

Adventureland's location within Disneyland was selected to take advantage of a row of eucalyptus trees used as a wind-break in the orange groves. Two tall, stately palm trees that once stood before the home of a pre-Disneyland owner, today blend into the tropic motif.

But Adventureland is more than trees and clinging vines. The Jungle River Cruise is a vicarious exploration for the stay-at-home dreamer, the adventurous spirit lurking somewhere in the hearts of all of us.

Many consider the Jungle River Cruise Disneyland's finest achievement. It compacts into a ten-minute experience the highlights, the *mystique* and excitement of a true-to-life adventure that could only be duplicated through weeks and months spent in the great outdoors. Source material for the designers was, in fact, gathered by photographers who did spend years in Africa—filming the Disney True-Life Adventure, "The African Lion."

Journey with 32 other passengers down tropic rivers, remote and mysterious, aboard bright canopied launches named for the world's waterways: *Mekong Maiden, Irrawaddy Woman, Ganges Gal.* Explore the misty rain-forest of the Amazon, the hippopotamus-filled waters of the Congo, the swirling rapids of the Nile. See a happy herd of elephants, "big shots and little squirts," playfully spraying each other with water and "showering" under a waterfall. Watch the survival of the fittest in the grasslands filled with zebras and lions, jackals and giraffe. See the plight of the "trapped safari," chased up a tree by a snorting, short-tempered, near-sighted rhinoceros, while hyenas laugh their approval.

An Adventureland safari is nearly as wide-ear as wide-eye; for the "native guides" who pilot the boats keep up a constant stream of chatter, part rehearsed and part ad-libbed, but all in the true spirit of adventure and fun. "Please remove your earrings," they warn the ladies. "They attract the head-hunters." Or, "Keep your hands and arms inside the boat — these crocodiles are always looking for a hand-out." And, "Gentlemen, if your mother-in-law is still aboard, you've missed a golden opportunity."

It is the type of dialogue that could be as precarious as a real-life jungle excursion.

That it succeeds is a tribute to that unique combination of living plants and life-like elephants, lions, hippos and gorillas—all members of a "cast" which has revolutionized entertainment. Adventureland, with its three-dimensional animated animals, was the laboratory where this revolution began, and continues.

In relative terms, it is a simple task to plan a mechanism for a special effect in a motion picture, one that will do a job once, twice or three times. But to design and build a machine that will produce the desired results and work reliably 12 or 14 hours a day, every day, is quite another story. And Disneyland's animals perform day and night. The jungle animals often startle guests by their realistic appearance and performance. The animals are amazingly complicated. At times, the maintenance crew has been known to say that "these alligators are more trouble than real ones!"

Seen from a front-row seat in a river packet, the Jungle River Cruise is tangible, personal adventure. Viewed from 70 feet above, the twisting waterway is serenity itself. The high vantage point is afforded by the largest of a rare, unnatural species of tree—the *Disneyodendron eximius,* an "out-of-the-ordinary Disney tree." Named for and designed after the Swiss Family Robinson's West Indies domain, its concrete roots penetrate 42 feet into the ground and 300,000 red vinyl leaves "grow" on its branches. Guests who climb to its top (stairs are thoughtfully provided) enjoy not only a wondrous view, but may tour the three-level Swiss Family Robinson tree house, examining the furniture and fixtures used in the parents' room, the boys' room and the delightful open-air "parlor."

A second fantastic *Disneyodendron eximus* towers high above the Tahitian Terrace. The terrace itself is an extraordinary stage setting whose curtain is a cascade of water, and whose footlights are leaping flames of fire burning on the water. The highlight of summer evening there comes when the falls magically draw aside, and from behind the waters sarong-clad natives appear to perform the swaying rhythms and rituals of the islands, the hypnotic barefoot fire walk, or the traditional grass-skirted dances of Samoa, Tahiti and Hawaii.

As they say in the travelogues, this too is Adventureland.

Frontierland

On a huge sound stage at the Disney studio in 1955, the era of Samuel Clemens' America was being reborn. For the first time in over half a century, a sternwheel steamboat was being built in the United States: a triple-deck paddlewheeler, appropriately to be christened *Mark Twain.* Soon it would ply a muddy Mississippi of its own, but in the early stages of construction, the riverboat's greatest claim to fame was as real-life proof of an old joke about the man who built a boat in his basement—and couldn't get it out the door.

The *Mark Twain,* 105 feet long, 150 tons and designed to carry 350 passengers, was indeed too big to move through the doors of even the giant sound stage—in its entirety. But this "queen of the river" was rather an unusual vessel: it was the first ever *prefabricated* sternwheeler—built in sections to be dismantled, trucked over freeways piece by piece, and reassembled at Disneyland!

Much of America's history is the story of frontiers awaiting conquest. To Walt Disney, a keen student of history, Disneyland could not be complete unless it told the story of America's pioneer development. As Walt has said, "All of us, whether tenth generation or naturalized Americans, have cause to be proud of our country's history, shaped by the pioneering spirit of our forefathers. It is to those hardy pioneers, men and women of vision, faith and courage, that we have dedicated Frontierland."

Disneyland's frontier stretches from the 1790's to the 1870's, and within the log stockade that serves as its entrance, touches on some of the most colorful aspects of American pioneer history: the boisterous frontier of Davy Crockett, the southwest with its rollicking dance halls, the charm and elegance of early New Orleans, the captivating lure of the ghost towns, and the romance of Tom Sawyer's Mississippi.

Like many a frontier town a century ago, Frontierland is built along a river, the half-mile long "Rivers of America." It was for travel on this waterway that the *Mark Twain* was re-created. Today it is, literally, one of the world's busiest rivers.

Here sails the *Columbia,* exact full-size replica of the first American ship to circumnavigate the globe (1787-1790). Built in Disneyland's own dry dock, this full-rigged, three-masted ship is the first such vessel constructed since the Civil War. It is a marvel of precise craftsmanship, right down to its "dead-eyes" and to the cotton and tar oakum used in hand-caulking its decks.

Here cruise the Mike Fink Keelboats and Indian war canoes that depart from the birch bark longhouse and ceremonial dancing circle of Disneyland's Indian Village. Guided by full-blooded Indians, these canoes furnish Disneyland's most active participation: personal paddling.

Here log rafts float from the mainland to another world—Tom Sawyer Island. Located in the middle of the River, the Island offers an adventure straight out of Samuel Clemens. It is complete with suspension and barrel bridges, Fort Wilderness, balancing and teetering rocks, Injun Joe's Cave and even fishing (for real perch and blue gill, pole and tackle free of charge).

Bordering the river is a composite True-

Life Adventure, based on elements of four Disney films, three of them Academy-Award winners. "Beaver Valley," "Bear Country," "The Living Desert" and "The Olympic Elk" provided the inspiration for this seven-acre attraction called Nature's Wonderland. So realistic are the 200 life-like animals, birds and reptiles that the migratory birds which fly over Disneyland have often attacked the animated ravens and owls. With its forest, desert and mountains, with "Old Unfaithful Geyser" spouting water 70 feet in the air, and with its colorful Rainbow Caverns, Nature's Wonderland is indeed the early western wilderness, re-born for a later western civilization.

Tomorrowland

Reactions of Russian visitors to Disneyland have always been closely followed by America's communications media. Photographers covering the tour of the Moscow Symphony Orchestra, anxious to obtain a picture of the Soviets near the Rocket to the Moon, conveyed their request through an interpreter. Animated discussion among the Russians followed, then a chorus of laughter and the interpreter's return. "They want to know," he dead-panned, "whether Walt Disney will guarantee the return trip."

Several years ago, in *Ford Times* magazine, Art Linkletter wrote: "On my House Party show, I frequently ask the kids if they've been to Disneyland, and if so, what they like best. One youngster told me, 'I like the scary rides, like the Matterhorn Bobsled Run; but Daddy always takes me on the submarines—he likes the mermaids!'"

These stories tell a tale of Tomorrowland:

here science-factual lives, but the un-science of tongue-in-cheek sometimes tiptoes close behind.

Originally, Tomorrowland's goal was to present "a living blueprint of our future." Of all Disneyland's realms, Tomorrowland was the most difficult to conceive and design, and it has undergone the most change. For Walt Disney and his artists were working not in the devil-may-care world of science fiction, but in one based upon conceptions of tomorrow held by some of America's foremost men of science and industry. And in the world we live in, what is tomorrow *today* is seldom tomorrow *tomorrow*.

"Lasers," "fly-bys," "communications satellites"—such terms and the technology to achieve them were unknown in 1954, when Tomorrowland was originally designed. Even the household word "astronaut" was still to be coined. Tomorrowland *has* been a success with Disneyland guests, however. A prime reason is that experts acted as advisors in the precarious business of predicting.

When Walt Disney determined Tomorrowland must have a science-factual flight to the moon, he enlisted two of America's outstanding authorities as the star-gazers: Dr. Wernher Von Braun, then chief of the U. S. Guided Missile Development Division; and Willy Ley, space travel expert.

Several years earlier, in a national magazine article, they had predicted the moon *could* be reached in ten years. Disneyland's simulated space flight, however, was not conceived as a space voyage of one or two astronauts, but rather a scheduled space flight that blasts off at regular intervals, circles the lunar body without landing, and then returns to the safe harbor of Disneyland's Spaceport.

Von Braun and Ley projected such flights *could* be routine by 1980. Taking the basic data they supplied, the Disney staff applied all the skills of motion picture special effects to create the proper moon-scape and in-flight views. Five years later their task would have been immeasurably more simple; in 1954, no film of actual blast-off was available, nor was there photography of the Earth from satellites in space. Every facet of the trip had to be realistically simulated.

Today, in the shadow of an 80-foot rocket ship, space travelers engulfed in sound effects and gently shaken by seat vibration simulating take-off and landing, participate in the early realization of one tomorrow. So accurate have the predictions been that the astounding events of a dozen years have required only the addition of satellites in orbit

and "fly-by" space ships.

In Tomorrowland the far reaches of outer space are but moments away from the distant depths of liquid space. On the Submarine Voyage, on a typical Disneyland day, thousands of visitors pass within touching distance of 24-karat gold valued at thousands of dollars. But the treasure in glittering urns and trinkets has its own built-in safeguards: first, it is under ten feet of water and second, it is protected by sharks, octopi, electric eels and even a sea serpent.

The gold is on view in the Submarine Voyage, a $2,500,000 journey to the bottom of the sea, where neophyte mariners chart a course aboard the grey-hulled vessels of, numerically, the world's eighth largest undersea fleet. Disneyland's submersibles, scale versions of America's nuclear-powered navy,

sail daily through a South Seas coral lagoon, beneath the Polar Ice Cap, through an underwater earthquake in the Lost Continent of Atlantis, past barnacle-laden Venetian galleys in the graveyard of sunken ships, and into a mermaid lagoon.

To enjoy the vast wonderworld at the bottom of the sea, each of 38 submarine passengers has his own individual porthole. Nearby, to preview the future of mass rapid transit, 106 seated passengers travel at speeds up to 45 miles per hour aboard trains of the Disneyland-Alweg Monorail System.

Early in the planning for Disneyland Walt Disney expressed interest in a "train of the future" for Tomorrowland. In 1957, following a visit to Cologne, Germany, the engineering staff recommended a design that appeared to offer the best prospects for economy, stability and all-around practicability, not only for Disneyland but for municipal transportation in general. Within two years Disneyland had become the first city in America to introduce a passenger-carrying monorail operating on a daily schedule.

Electrically powered, running on rubber tires over a concrete beamway, a highway in the sky, these almost silent trains immediately captured the public's fancy. Within two years the entire system was extended outside Disneyland for a practical transportation purpose: carrying passengers between the Disneyland Hotel and Tomorrowland's station.

Today the Disneyland-Alweg Monorail System is two and a half miles long, parallels a major highway and crosses a city street. Basic design of its three trains, including power, brake and safety systems, could easily be used in metropolitan transit.

Monorail is a very old idea, not a new phenomenon. Since 1901 Wuppertal, Germany, has had a suspended monorail in which cars ride under the beam—in contrast to the straddling, piggy-back style of Disneyland's. But in an age when urban transit problems are "cussed and discussed" almost daily, Walt Disney was pioneering once again with a showcase for public examination and enjoyment. As an executive of a major transportation company said later, "You've built this entire system in less time, and for about the same money, that my company would allocate for a *feasibility* study!"

How has Tomorrowland, that "living blueprint of our future," fared in practice? In some ways, quite successfully. For one, it has proved to be an ideal framework for displays by American industry. Monsanto's House of the Future indicates a potential new dimension for the use of plastics in housing. The

Circarama, the 360-degree motion picture technique premiered at Disneyland in 1955, has already contributed to an understanding of the U.S. through showings of *America the Beautiful* at the Brussels World's Fair, a United States Exhibit in Moscow, and other fairs. Audiences watch its encircling film from the center of the action so that they may see, almost simultaneously, in front and behind them, and all the scenery in between.

Even the narrow ribbons of roads which make up Autopia's freeways, with multi-levels, criss-crosses and divided one-way lanes, were a prediction of things to come in 1955. Few states in America had an ultra-modern expressway system to match Disneyland's in those days.

When Disneyland opened, experts on road construction and safety no doubt found Autopia interesting. Over the years, however, it is the student of human nature who has been most intrigued by this miniature turnpike system. For, side by side with youngsters gaining their first experience behind the wheel of a real gasoline powered auto, the same adults who grumble and fume about traffic on southern California's full-size freeways plunge happily into Autopia's junior size traffic jams in scaled-down sports cars. Obviously, tomorrow *can* be a wonderful age.

Kings are Commoners and Commoners are Kings

Today the magic of the name Disney and the magnet of the place Disneyland extend from the court rooms of Texas to the gilded courts of Europe's royal families.

In San Antonio, Texas, a prospective juror told the learned judge that he was perfectly

Bell System has used Disneyland for the first major public demonstrations of the picture phone and the family phone booth. Douglas' moon flight has contributed to public understanding of distant space travel.

Tomorrowland has showcased several important new developments. The piggy-back type monorail may have an unlimited metropolitan future. As writer Robert DeRoos said in the *National Geographic,* "Most passengers, myself included, leave the monorail convinced it is the answer for rapid transit of the future."

willing to serve, but he had already made plans to take his six children to Disneyland. Noting that he had "made a similar commitment for this year," the judge ruled without hesitation: juror excused!

The Louisville (Kentucky) *Courier-Journal* editorialized: "Foreign tourists should not be frightened away by reports of excessive red tape in the United States. It is not true, for example, that a separate visa is required for Disneyland."

The Park has been called "a land where kings are commoners and commoners are kings." Part of this designation is explained by the long list of VIP's numbered among Disneyland's visitors. Kings and queens who have been guests include Morocco's Mohammed V, Jordan's Hussein, Belgium's Baudouin, Nepal's Mahendra and Queen Ratna, Thailand's Bhumibol and Queen Sirikit, Denmark's Frederick IX and Queen Ingrid, Afghanistan's Mohamed Zaher and Queen

"'Customer' is a bad word.

"We are hosts and hostesses, and *everyone* who enters our main gate is a guest!"

Some Disneyland visitors, however, have had difficulty being just plain guests in the Magic Kingdom. Everywhere motion picture star Betty Hutton went in Disneyland, visitors recognized her and asked for autographs. So Miss Hutton determined to disguise herself. Spying Merlin's Magic Shop in Fantasyland, she purchased a clever concealment—long, false eyelashes, a buccaneer's hat and a special "sword" that appeared to go right through her head. The disguise worked perfectly. No one recognized Miss Hutton. But people continued to stop her. This time they weren't interested in autographs. They wanted to know where they could buy "a hat like that crazy one you've got on!"

"The Greatest Show On Earth"

It was old P. T. Barnum who called the circus "The Greatest Show on Earth." In Barnum's day, none could dispute him—the circus reigned supreme. Today, the lure of the circus has paled; the ballyhoo of Barnum has faded into the past. When people talk of "the greatest show on earth," chances are they're talking about Disneyland.

We live in an age of increasing mechanization. Certainly the technology of the space age, applied to entertainment, has been the most fascinating new tool of Disney imagineers over the past decade. But paradoxically, while new animated arts have flourished in Disneyland, the Magic Kingdom has also conceived its own brand of three-ring, something's-always-happening excitement. Live en-

Hemaira, and the Shah of Iran. Presidents and prime ministers, several dozen princes and princesses, assorted United Nations delegates, U.S. senators and congressmen, governors, mayors and a full complement of Hollywood stars and their families have visited the Park.

However, the fundamental reason for the king-commoner analogy is found in the basic approach to entertaining its guests that is practiced at Disneyland. Here employees strive to live up to a credo contained in the Park's training manual: "We love to entertain kings and queens, but the vital thing to remember is this: *Every* guest receives the VIP treatment."

Appropriately entitled, "You're on Stage at Disneyland," the training booklet establishes a number of bywords:

"It's not just important to be friendly and courteous to the public, it's essential . . .

tertainment is, perhaps, the most surprising success in today's "greatest show."

Back in 1955, Pepsi Cola's Golden Horseshoe Revue presented a light and gay musical revue. The Disneyland Band tooted in parades and concerts. The spaceman quickly became the focus of all cameras. Today, each is still going strong; the Golden Horseshoe, in fact, is America's longest-running show, after more than 18,000 performances. But the contrast between 1955 and Disneyland's live entertainment today is staggering.

On weekend and summer afternoons in the 1960's, mountain climbers scale the Matterhorn. Along Main Street a barber shop quartet harmonizes—aboard a bicycle-built-for-four. In Frontierland Indian dances compete with the guitar-strumming rhythms of a Mexican trio and the jazz of a Dixieland band. In Fantasyland dozens of Disney characters—Mickey Mouse, Pluto, the Three Little Pigs

and Big Bad Wolf, Snow White and the Seven Dwarfs—come to life in people-size costumes. In Tomorrowland spaceman and spacegirl greet earthlings, large and small. And back in Frontierland town marshal and outlaw continue to duel, six-gun style.

On a summer's eve the Fantasy-in-the-Sky fireworks bursting over Disneyland signal the start of southern California's most diverse night life. Dance bands swing out with everything from the twisting, rocking rhythms of the teens to the fox trot, two-beat Dixieland and the swaying melodies of the Pacific Islands. The Park has kept pace with the always-changing trends in teen-age music; the hootenany has found a home here, as have the rousing spirituals of gospel choirs.

Yet Disneyland, on a summer evening, is a mecca for adults, too. Offered the right atmosphere, people will still come out to dance to the big bands. Today, Disneyland presents

a whole series of special nighttime events: Dixieland at Disneyland, big band nights, weekend and holiday festivals, and the world's largest New Year's Eve party, where 19,000 annually toast the past and coming years — with non-alcoholic beverages.

For teen-agers, the park has become a date night destination. Special evenings include a frantic Spring Fling and four high school Grad Nights at which 60,000 seniors from 160 schools dance and laugh and cry in all-night celebrations.

But while special entertainment and big name stars often gather the headlines, the newest and biggest everyday star at Disneyland is *Audio-Animatronics*.

So named because it ingeniously combines sound and animation with space-age electronics, Audio-Animatronics made its debut in 1963 in the Enchanted Tiki Room. Here, in a sit-down theater show, more than 225 birds and flowers (none of them alive) and tropic Tiki idols sing, talk, joke and chant in life-like fashion.

Disney technicians have devised a complex way to program movements and record them — along with music, singing, dialogue and sounds — on a single, one-inch magnetic tape. Hundreds of separate actions can be programmed and stored on this tape. When the recorded animation and music is played back, electronic impulses activate air cylinders, pis-

By Thomas Nebbia ©National Geographic Society

tons, springs and valves inside the figures. Magically, birds talk, Tikis chant and flowers croon.

The Tiki Room would have been an impossibility in 1955, when Disneyland opened. It took the precision techniques and electronic systems of the space age to produce the revue. Or, as one technician puts it, "We've got almost enough gadgets and equipment for this show to put all of Disneyland into orbit!"

"Disneyland Will Never Be Completed"

When Disneyland opened, Walt Disney told a nation-wide television audience: "Disneyland will never be completed. It will continue to grow, to add new things, as long as there is imagination left in the world."

Even as the first crowds poured into the Park, Walt Disney was planning for the future. "Walt has the daring, the audacity to stake his personal reputation on something he believes in — and to visualize what it will be like when completed," observes an associate. "Other people would have said, 'We've spent $17 million and we sure hope it's successful so we can get our money back'. But Walt was saying, 'It cost $17 million, people will have fun, and next year we'll add...'"

"Next year we'll add..." No single phrase more clearly sums up the story of Disneyland since its debut. By the mid-1960's, the park that was "something of a fair, a city from the Arabian nights" had become a $75 million international playground visited by citizens of more than 100 nations, and annually attracting more than six million patrons, over four million of them adults. Originally it had 22 attractions; today there are more than 50.

An entire new land, New Orleans Square, has grown up on the banks of the Rivers of America. Total price tag of these new adventures: more than *three times* Disneyland's initial cost.

Oddly enough, the 1964-65 New York World's Fair, more than 3,000 miles from Anaheim, has brought about more changes in the Magic Kingdom than any other single stimulant.

The story of Disney-at-the-Fair also began at WED Enterprises. There, often side-by-side with new ideas for Disneyland, World's Fair attractions for General Electric, Pepsi Cola, Ford Motor Company and the State of Illinois were conceived and designed.

For two springs and summers in New York,

Disneyland-style entertainment captivated eastern audiences. Ninety-one percent of the Fair's paid attendance—46,871,236 people—visited these four Disney attractions.

Today, the story of Disney and the Fair continues. After a two year "road show" in New York, all four shows, in one form or another, are finding new homes in Disneyland. In 1965, the Magic Kingdom unveiled the first of these Fair attractions, "Great Moments with Mr. Lincoln."

Walt Disney has long held the belief, shared by many Americans, that more of us should recognize the influence of historical events on our lives today...and the significance of our American heritage in the future development of this nation. That belief motivated "Great Moments with Mr. Lincoln."

Presented in a new 500-seat theater in Town Square's Opera House, this stirring dramatization has at its heart the three-dimensional figure of Abraham Lincoln.

The Lincoln figure is a true work of art, a blending of ancient and modern crafts. Ten years of research and thousands of man hours by artists, sculptors and skilled technicians — experts in the new field of Audio-Animatronics — went into the creation of this incredibly life-like representation of America's sixteenth president. The figure rises from a chair and addresses the Disneyland audience in the words of the Great Emancipator — words as applicable today as they were a century ago:

"Let us have faith that right makes might," counsels Lincoln, "and in that faith, let us, to the end, dare to do our duty as we understand it."

It is a presentation worthy of its name, "...a different and exciting way to stress history's importance to each of us," in the words of Walt Disney.

History of a vastly different sort, some of it pre-dating man on earth, provided the themes for two of Disneyland's major additions in the $20 million expansion of 1966. One is the Primeval World.

Boarding trains of the Santa Fe & Disneyland Railroad, guests first travel through the Grand Canyon diorama, then are whisked back in time many millions of years to a day when giant creatures thundered over the land or soared like gliders across the sky. In the

Primeval World, brontosaurus, stegosaurus, pterodactyl, triceratops and the frightening king of all the dinosaurs, tryannosaurus, "come to life" through Audio-Animatronics.

These giant reptiles, ranging in height up to 15 feet, actually roamed the North American continent. In Disneyland, both the vegetarian brontosaurus and carnivorous tyrannosaurus, life-size and life-like, once more rule an earth changing from misty swampland to fiery, erupting volcanoes.

Historical fact and a dash of dashing fable

also influenced Walt and his WED staff in the creation of New Orleans Square and its major adventure the Pirates of the Caribbean.

In both atmosphere and architecture, New Orleans Square recreates the Crescent City in its golden age a century ago. Along its winding streets and in sheltered courtyards are Disneyland's most distinctive adventures in shopping and dining. Literally years of research and study went into the planning; out of this attention to detail and desire to recreate the classic traditions of old New Orleans came a series of "showcases." Here,

in a land as large as Main Street, each shop and restaurant is one "act" in a thematic adventure; each dramatizes — in sight, in sound, in antique merchandise — one part of the exciting legend that was New Orleans, vintage 1850.

There is *Mlle. Antoinette's Parfumerie*, with mirrors that revive the lost art of painting in reverse; the decorations are painted first, and the mirrors are silvered only after the artist has completed his painstaking work. *The Creole Cafe* is distinguished by its tile floor and zinc-top coffee bar; espresso is served

here from an ancient steam machine admired and purchased in Milan by Walt Disney. *Le Gourmet* offers hard-to-find culinary accessories, while the brick-walled *French Market* attracts diners with two tile murals depicting early New Orleans. And the exciting *Blue Bayou Restaurant* serves *poulet, crevettes, boeuf* and *poisson* by candlelight, which is only proper in a setting where moonlight shines all day long, Mardi Gras entertainment reigns, and the sight of the Bayou creates a mood at once mysterious and adventurous.

To find adventure of a totally different kind in New Orleans Square is to walk along Royal St., down Front St. into Pirate Alley. There, at the end of the quay, flat-bottom *bateaux* take on their seafaring guests, then glide serenely across the Blue Bayou Lagoon. Sud-

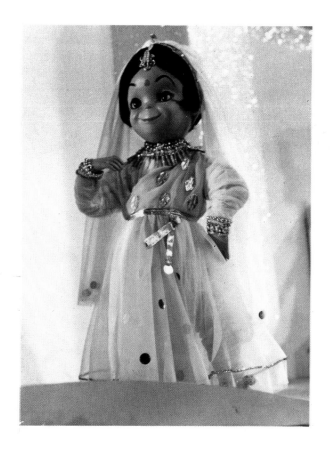

denly the boats plunge down a steep waterfall into the lair of the Pirates of the Caribbean.

"Avast there mates — ye that be young in heart! It's the gold of the New World we be searchin' for!" And you, vicarious visitor, are there, too — together with some of the wildest scoundrels who ever sailed the Spanish Main. A crew of dozens, all Audio-Animatronic, venture forth, cannons blazing and cutlasses drawn, to loot and plunder a port village.

On the other side of the Park, in Fantasyland, is another boat ride new to Disneyland in 1966. It's the happiest cruise that ever sailed 'round the globe: "It's a Small World."

Against stylized and colorful backgrounds of six continents, Audio-Animatronic children of more than 100 nations (all in colorful native costumes) sing and dance and weave the magic spell that charmed more than ten million people at the World's Fair. Toys and animals join the fun too; from the first chorus to the final fling, this is a merry fantasy of childhood expressed in the words of the title tune: "Though the mountains divide and the oceans are wide, it's a small world...after all!"

Disneyland's gaudiest marquee—the world's happiest clock, standing 30-feet high — calls visitors to It's A Small World. This wacky and whimsical clock actually *performs* the time, pulsating and vibrating and seemingly ready to explode...until the blare of trumpeting toy soldiers and a parade of toys from around the world announces each quarter hour.

In many ways, the happy spirit of It's A Small World expresses the *joie de vivre* of Disneyland and its chief architect. For even as these new adventures opened in 1966, Walt Disney was finalizing plans for additions just as ambitious, to open in 1967. The major

change: a new Tomorrowland.

Catalyst for this new area is American industry. Here the General Electric "Carousel of Progress," another World's Fair hit show, will find a new home; Monsanto will welcome guests on a trip into the micro-world of the atom; Douglas will spirit earthmen on a flight to outer space; and the Bell System will tour America in a new Circlevision production of "America the Beautiful."

But perhaps new Tomorrowland can best be placed in perspective through its "spaceport" and theme center, home base for four-passenger rocket ships that will simulate the sensation of racing through distant space. Spiraling as high as an 18-story building, this towering structure will be visible for miles — a gleaming metallic mountain — the biggest single structure ever built in Disneyland.

What Is Not Yet Done

More than a century ago, the famous French author Alexis de Tocqueville heard the heartbeat of a new nation.

"America is a land of wonders," he wrote, "in which everything is in constant motion, and every change seems an improvement. No natural boundary seems to be set to the efforts of man; and in his eyes what is not yet done is only what he has not yet attemped to do."

What de Tocqueville wrote about America a hundred years ago could easily be said of Disneyland today. As Walt himself has said:

"I believe the fun is in building something, in bringing new things to life. We never do the same thing twice. After we've finished a job around here we head in another direction. We're always opening up new doors."

PRINTED IN ITALY BY OFFICINE GRAFICHE ARNOLDO MONDADORI - VERONA